JAMAICA

JAMAICA

Copyright© 1984—Ray Chen.
ALL RIGHTS RESERVED.
Second re-print 1987.

No part of this book may be reproduced in any
form or by any electronic or mechanical
means including information storage and
retrieval systems without permission in writing
from the publisher, except by a reviewer who
may quote brief passages in a review.

Published by
Ray Chen
1420, rue Notre-Dame ouest,
Montréal (Québec) Canada.
H3C 1K9   Tél: (514) 931-2203

5 Union Square
Kingston 5, Jamaica
(809) 92-91516/92-92625

Canadian Cataloguing in Publication Data.

Includes index.
ISBN 0-9691792-0-0

Chen, Ray - 1939 -
1. Jamaica - Description and travel - 1984 - Views.
(i) The Land   (ii) The People

Printed and bound in Hong Kong
By Scanner Art Services Inc., Toronto

For Lin with much love,
Ray

ACKNOWLEDGEMENTS:

To His Excellency The Most Honourable Sir Florizel Glasspole, ON, G.C.M.G., G.C.V.O., C.D., LLD (HON) Governor General of Jamaica.

Thank you for your kind words of introduction.

To Mr. Lascelles Chin, "a very special thank you" for his enthusiasm, interest and tremendous assistance which he gave in so many ways. In the early stage, his introduction to Mr. John Gentles, the past Director of the Jamaica Tourist Board, and to its many members of staff, was a blessing. For without their expert knowledge, assistance, and most of all, their encouragement, it would have been more difficult in some areas to have photographic work done. The present Director, Miss Carrole Guntley, and her staff, have continued to be a source of encouragement and especially Mr. Anthony (Tony) King: a big Thank You.

And to these individuals who gave so generously of themselves, their knowledge and their time. Merci, merci, beaucoup.

Mr. James P.R. Doyle for his valuable help from day one and his talent in designing a format to fill the need for the many images.

Mr. Robert Lee for sharing more than his home with me during my stay on the island.

Irene Mayo for lending more than an ear. She has listened to my thoughts, and has put words to what I have expressed in my photos.

To Wayne Chen and Anna Gedalof for being such good listeners, someone to talk with when the going got tough.

To Rick and Stephanie, for their encouragement and support, especially during my long absence from home.

And a sincere thanks to these wonderful friends, old and new, for their hospitality, kindness and help.

Yolanda Sabdul, Carol Samuel, Lola Hohn, Byron Henry (Jamaica Tourist Board).

Captain E.C. Alliman (J.D.F.), David Boxer (National Gallery), Geoff Cannon, Monica Chen, Vincent and Gloria Chen, Joe and Lucia Chin, Jean Delisle, Barbara Gloudon (Little Theatre Movement), Inspector Noel Gordon (Jamaica Police Academy), Edmond and Paulette Hew, Rosita Johnson Dance Troupe, Benjamin Koo, Coraine and Desmond Lee, Captain J.E. Lewin (J.D.F.), Caroline Lewis, Peter Packer, Barbara Requa (Jamaica School of Dance), James Rickard, Vera A. Stacey, David Steiner, Floyd Weekes (for the long hours), Patrick and Yvonne Yap.

I also wish to thank all the wonderful people of the island for their time, their hospitality and most of all for allowing me to photograph them, including those who are not shown in this book. You are true Jamaicans, and I love you all. Because of you... A Dream has become a reality.

JAMAICA - A DREAM

Three years have passed since I started my quest to fulfill a dream - a pictorial essay on the island. Having lived away for almost twenty years, and only visiting the island for holidays, I often felt like a visitor. It was days before I overcame that silly thought, and settled down into being a Jamaican again. In some way, the feeling of being a visitor made me aware that there were many things which, as Jamaicans, we took for granted. Based on these feelings, I was determined to capture on film these places and people so that they would never be lost to us.

It was difficult deciding where to start, but since we were to show the island in two parts, The Land and The People - it made certain decisions easier. Once started, I realized that there had been many changes, and so I anticipated each coming day with more enthusiasm and excitement. There was no stopping now, so much to be done!

As I journeyed the length and breadth of our island, I was aware that there were still many parts which very few Jamaicans have seen, and as a visitor it was even more impossible to see it all in a short stay. One does not realize how mountainous an island it is, though this is quite apparent from the air, and a bird's-eye view of the coral reefs takes on another dimension. I was awed by the physical layout of the Cockpit

Country, and often as we came to the end of one ride, I took time to reflect on what I had just finished photographing. Areas of extreme opposites exist on this small island. Two examples are the lush vegetation in the Parish of Portland and the dry desert-like condition of Sandy Bank in St. Elizabeth. To compare the white sandy beach of Negril (Westmoreland) to the pebble-covered beach of Morant Bay (St. Thomas) is another fine example.

Travelling by road through the valleys and mountains proved to be equally breathtaking, though stopping by the roadside to admire the landscape in a vehicle can be a little tricky as the roads tend to be quite narrow.

It is these same roads that take you through the towns, villages and cities of our island. It is here that you meet some of the friendliest people in the land, who will always have a warm, welcoming smile to greet you, a total stranger.

For the very brief period that it took to do a photograph and have a little chat, it became very obvious how proud we are to be Jamaican. It was therefore important for me to show Jamaicans as they really are, and to do so, my travels took me into many homes, offices, factories, shops, sugar plantations and churches. I have always been fascinated by the different religions and customs of our churches, and it was to find these that I travelled many miles, trying to track down certain activities. The street-corner meeting in Bamboo, St. Ann, will always be a mysterious, exciting experience at sundown, as will the bright, refreshing feeling that comes from a midday service in Walderston (Manchester). Listening to the drums and chanting on a Sunday night will always give me goose bumps and remind me of my happy childhood.

The school children continue to remind us of our carefree days, as does visiting the Candy Lady with all the goodies in her little wooden box... coconut gizada, grater-cake, cut cake, peppermint candy and sweet potato pudding. Mangoes, guinep, starapple, naseberry and otaheite apple are just a few of the fruits that I enjoyed having in the car while travelling. I especially liked a freshly cut "coconut water", fried fish by the beach with enough pepper to bring tears to my eyes.

The fruits are always in abundance and are constantly changing with the seasons. So do the flowers which surround us every day, in all the colours of the rainbow. Maybe this is reflected in the colourful manner in which we dress and for this reason, I especially enjoyed photographing my "new friends."

Politicians, police, housewives, businessmen, fishermen, rastamen, our beautiful women, their homes and their lifestyles, the mountains, rivers and valleys... all helped to make this book possible.

The photography was not an easy task, and I must admit it was even more difficult to make the final selection. I wanted to show Jamaica to the rest of the World - images that make us so very different - as well as why we are proud of our country, proud to be called Jamaicans.

I realize that it will take more than one book to show all of Jamaica, but if in some way these photos help to convey the beauty and soul of Jamaica, then I will have succeeded in my goal. I hope you will enjoy them as much as I have enjoyed photographing and sharing them with you.

Ray Chen

INTRODUCTION

I am pleased to have been asked to do the introduction to this pictorial essay because as a born and bred native son, it delights me to see the island presented from so many refreshing angles.

This book started and ended as an emotional pilgrimage for the photographer, Ray Chen, who himself is a Jamaican. He literally left no stone unturned, no road untravelled, as he criss-crossed the island in order to catch Jamaicans in their most candid moments, pursuing their lives in our cities, mountains and villages. Every Jamaican whom Mr. Chen approached had time to stop... and smile, and this is reflected in the undisguised openess and genuine radiance of their expressions.

Jamaica is a natural subject for a photo essay: she has vibrant, living colours, an astonishing variety of flora and fauna - and the warmth of her people which leaps out from the pages, refusing to be confined in one-dimensional photographs.

Our country has undergone many historical, philosophical, economical and political changes. She has been a silent witness to slavery and independence, turmoil and peace, poverty and prosperity. Through it all, the island has evolved and emerged more secure and serene than ever. Yet, it remains a land with much left to be discovered. Just when we feel we have experienced her every nuance and mood, Jamaica manages to show us another facet of her ever-changing character.

I personally feel that Mr. Ray Chen has caught the flavour, excitement and tempo of life in Jamaica as it really is and frozen these moments forever on celluloid. Here between the pages, he has, with technical mastery and distinctive talent, expressed our national pride and universal appeal.

This production is one of a lasting record and will be well worth viewing.

I congratulate Mr. Chen and wish him success in this effort.

Florizel Glasspole

Governor General

Kings House
Kingston, Jamaica W.I.
Feb. 9, 1984

THE LAND
THE PEOPLE

Jamaica is the third largest island in the Caribbean Sea, with a land area of approximately 4,232 sq. miles (10,962 km²) -150 miles (260 km) long, by 50 miles (70 km) at its widest point. It has a population of just over 2 million, and the capital, Kingston, is the largest English-speaking city in the Caribbean and South America.

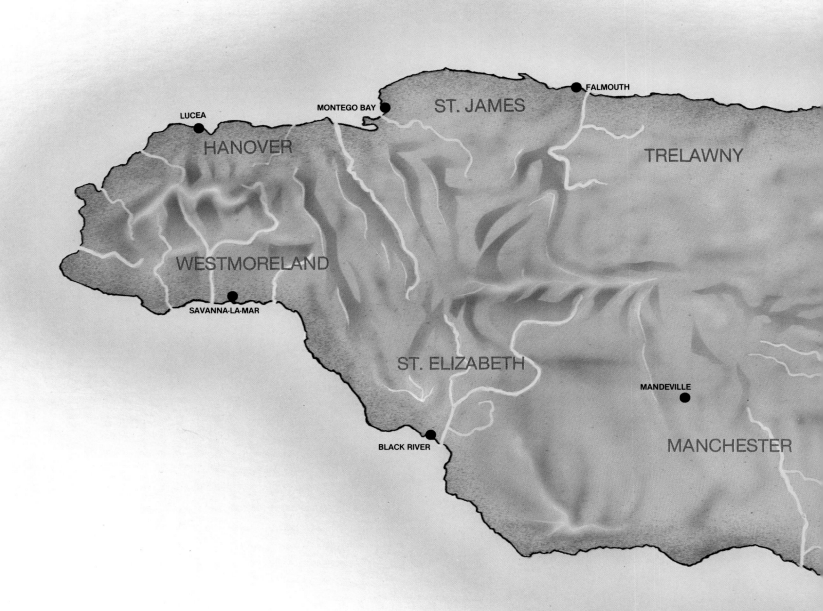

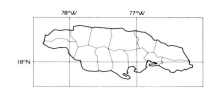

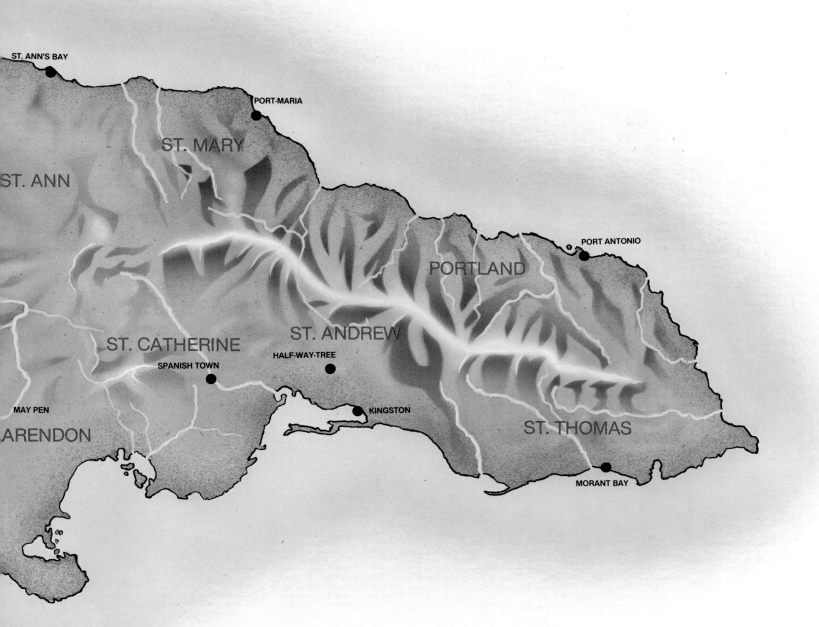

ST. ANN'S BAY

PORT-MARIA

ST. MARY

ST. ANN

PORT ANTONIO

PORTLAND

ST. ANDREW

ST. CATHERINE

HALF-WAY-TREE

SPANISH TOWN

MAY PEN

KINGSTON

ARENDON

ST. THOMAS

MORANT BAY

Colors of our flag: gold, black and green.

The gold stands for sunlight and mineral wealth, the black for hardships of the past and future, and the green for hope and agricultural wealth.

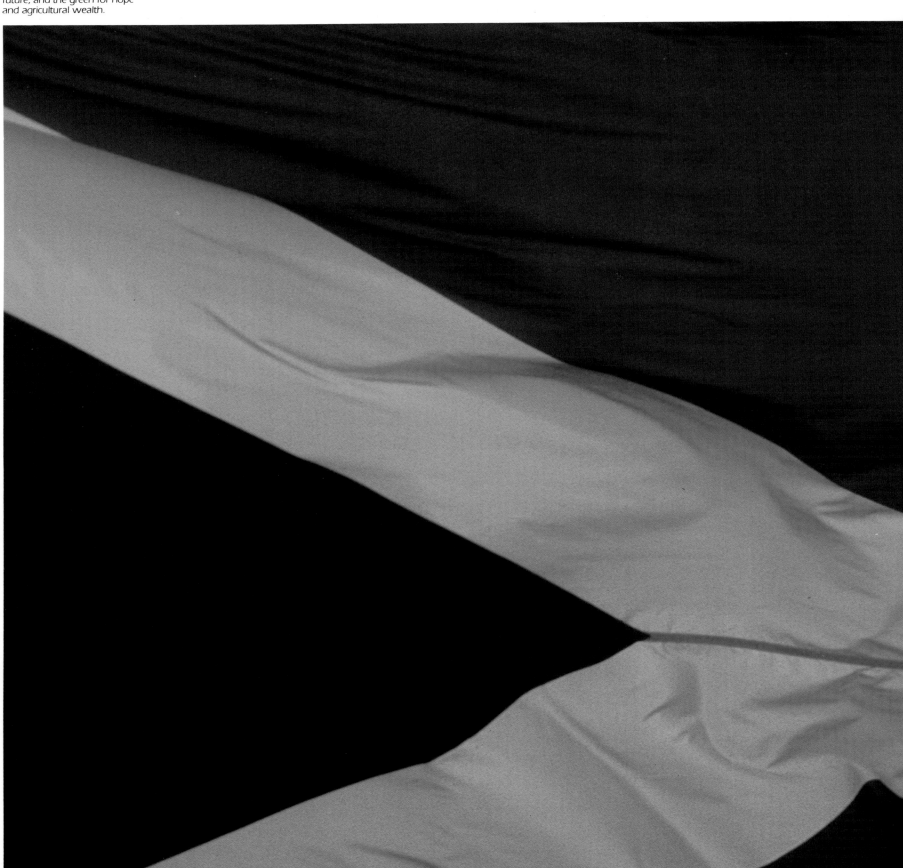

THE LAND

Jamaica - land of wood and water, blessed by cool, seductive breezes and lush vegetation. No other Caribbean island can rival the variety of her landscapes - from the tip of Blue Mountain Peak stretching almost a mile and a half into the sky, to the undulating valleys nestled below. The mountains are omnipresent. Solidly entrenched like a giant, writhing backbone, they reach out in every direction, stoney arms extended protectively to cup valleys and streams. They are the source of dozens of rivers which are fed by rains and mysterious underground springs. Like so many rambunctious children, they come gurgling and splashing over big and small boulders on their inevitable journey to the sea.

Where mountains meet coast line, great gusting winds push frothy waves onto the shore, and the salty air mixed with sand feels real and gritty between your teeth.

Portions of the island experience extremely high rainfalls, causing rivers to overflow with regularity and, in receding, leave the banks more lush and verdant than ever. One such river, the Rio Grande, is as well travelled as any Jamaican road. Well-muscled rafters take their passengers downstream on bamboo rafts towards the mouth of the river, past laughing, chattering women who wash their laundry in the river and spread them out on the rocks to dry. Transportation on the island comes in many shapes and sizes. Country buses ply the roads between villages, perpetually overcrowded. There is always one or two passengers hanging on precariously by the entrance. The tops of the buses serve another useful purpose: chickens, bags, suitcases, baskets of vegetables - all are tossed on the roof in a carefree, clinging heap.

It's a cheerful sight to see these buses as they careen around corners at a speed and rhythm only Jamaicans can understand. Since there are no sidewalks except in larger towns, all share the thoroughfare and each must fend for himself.

Near operating sugar plantations, tractors and overloaded trucks chug up and down, spilling large pieces of freshly cut cane all over the road. Sugar is one of Jamaica's key crops, as are bananas, citrus, pimento, cocoa, coconuts, ginger and tobacco. Secondary crops are pineapple, mango, pawpaw, guava, avocado pear, soursop, sweet sop, naseberry, ackee and jackfruit. Many of these grow wild and often all you have to do is step off the road and help yourself.

Jamaica's flowers and plants are also extraordinarily diverse. There are almost three thousand different kinds of plants which bear flowers and over five hundred kinds of ferns. Unique in their coloration and shapes, many are found only in Jamaica and nowhere else in the world. The names of towns give tantalizing hints of Jamaica's past. Some sound ferocious: Bloody Bay, Cutlass Point, Black River, Wreck Point, whereas others are decidedly whimsical: Wait-a-bit, Welsh Woman's Point, Friar's Cap Point, and Ginger Hill. Then there is the Land of Look-Behind located in the western centre of the island. The British tried to quell a band of Maroons in 1600, made up mostly of freed and runaway slaves, but they failed in their mission. The Maroons were crafty and seasoned fighters, quietly attacking the British from behind and then as quickly and silently, stealing away again. Today it is better known as the Cockpit Country and is still the home of the descendants of those original runaway slaves.

The central part of the island is riddled with many caves, and to reach them you must make the trip by train - since it's the only way to get to them. It's a satisfying experience, rewarded by unforgettable scenes of glistening walls and ceilings, and warm, secretive sounds.

To not speak of Jamaica's beaches would be an unforgivable oversight - to speak of them is to make a conscious effort at limiting the use of superlatives. Sugar-fine, shell-pink, beautiful, blinding in the sun... they've all been said. They are an experience no one should deny himself. The Caribbean Sea is an endless wonder. Warm and calm, restless and wild, safe and treacherous by turn, you learn to love it, always wanting to be near it, yet never completely trusting it. Its shades of blues, greens and turquoises defy description.

The ocean never evokes the same feeling in two people, and therein lies its mystery and its power.

So many exotic and soothing elements come together in Jamaica, that to be there is to awaken to a continuous sense of astonishment. It is to calmly accept the impossibility of so many rampant colours - yet still feel awed by the galactic explosion of a setting sun... no matter how often you've seen it before. It is to open all the senses dulled by too many sounds of civilization and feel a rush of new emotions, and not be ashamed to acknowledge them as being real and sincere.

● Dawn - Looking east from
Rose Hall.
St. James.

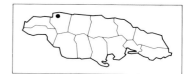

27

■ Sunset - at Folly.
Portland.

28

● Innswood Sugar Cane
Plantation between Spanish
Town and Old Harbour.
St. Catherine.

29

■ Dunn's River Falls.
Ocho Rios, St. Ann.

30

■ Early morning sunrise above
the Blue Mountains.
Kingston.

32

● Another view during the day
at Corn Puss Gap, St. Thomas.

33

■ A sugar cane plantation near
Serge Island.
St. Thomas.

● Newcastle Military Training
Camp nestling in the
mountains.
St. Andrew.

35

■ Unusual coastline near
Llandovery.
St. Ann.

● Checker-board farmlands
Clarendon.

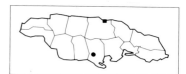

37

■ A line of trees cresting the
Blue Mountains.
"Telegraph Mountains",
St. Andrew.

38

● A private hide-a-way along
the coastline near
Manchioneal.
Portland.

■ The Santa-Cruz Mountains
seen from Savanna-la-Mar.
Westmoreland.

40

● Meeting point of the
Rio Grande and the Back
River, showing the
John Crow Mountains.
Portland.

41

■ Sunset.
Kingston.

43

44

Looking north on Knutsford
Boulevard.
New Kingston.

45

■ Devon House, Kingston.
Restored to its former
grandeur.

46

Devon House.
Twilight.

■ King's House.
Official residence of the
Governor General.
Liguanea, St. Andrew.

Vale Royal
Official residence of the
Prime Minister.
Liguanea, St. Andrew,

49

■ King Street.
Kingston.

50

Clock at Half-Way Tree.
St. Andrew.

■ National Heroes Park.
Kingston.

University of the West Indies.
Mona, St. Andrew.

53

■ Bird's eye view of coral reef.
St. James.

54

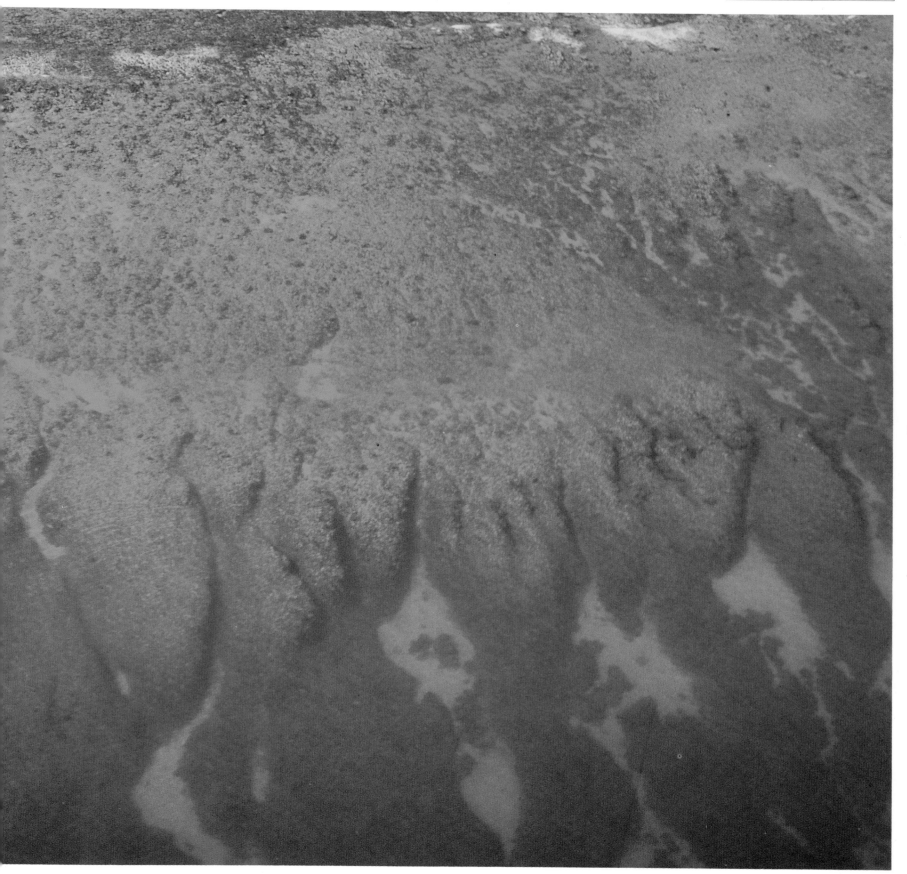

55

● North-coast resort beach.
Ocho Rios, St. Ann.

57

58

● Rocky coast along the eastern
 shores.
 Long Bay - Portland.

59

■ Sunrise at Montego Bay.
St. James.

60

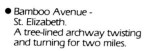

● Bamboo Avenue -
St. Elizabeth.
A tree-lined archway twisting
and turning for two miles.

61

■ Fern Gully, St. Ann.
A protected reserve where
one can see the many dif-
ferent species of fern growing
here.

62

● The Blue Mountain Peak as
seen from Duckensfield Hall.
St. Thomas.

63

● Rock House.
Holiday cottages along the cliff
at Negril.
Westmoreland.

65

■ Swimmers enjoying the water
at Doctor's Cave Beach.
Montego Bay, St. James.

66

■ Port Antonio - Portland.

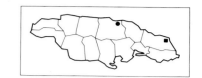

● "Couples."
Hotel in Ocho Rios.
St. Ann.

69

■ Lewis Galdy Tombstone -
St. Peter's Church
Port Royal.

Crest on cannon
Window in wall

Fort Charles. - Port Royal
"In this Place dwelt
Horatio Nelson."

71

■ Small country shop in
Philadelphia.
St. Ann.

72

● "Home Sweet Home."
Newell, St. Elizabeth.

73

Old Jamaican architecture.

Ocho Rios - St. Ann.
Montego Bay - St. James.
Port Antonio - Portland.

Handygrove District -
St. Elizabeth.
Porus - Manchester.
Port Antonio - Portland.

Savanna-la-Mar
-Westmoreland.
Ginger Hill - St. Ann.
Brown's Town - St. Ann.

74

● Railway station and railway
men at Buff Bay.
Portland.

75

■ Huts used for drying tobacco.
May Pen, Clarendon.

● Preparing the young coffee
plants for transplanting.
Silver Hill Gap, in the
Blue Mountains.
St. Andrew.

77

■ Ocho Rios, St. Ann.

■ Fishermen taking a break at
Oracabessa.
St. Mary.

● Fishermen's boats at
Treasure Beach.
St. Elizabeth.

■ Cable Hut Beach
looking towards Copacabana.
St. Thomas.

82

● Line fishing near the mouth of
the Morant River.
St. Thomas.

83

■ Old water wheel at the
Tryall Estate.
Hanover.

84

● Hope Gardens - St. Andrew. Established in 1873 on 200 acres of land, now known as the Royal Botanical Gardens.

85

■ Caves in the Cockpit Country.
Ipswich - St. Elizabeth.

86

● A wall of hibiscus plants on roadside.
Stony Hill, St. Andrew.

87

■ Desert like land at Sandy Bank.
St. Elizabeth.

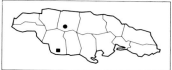

● Aerial view of
Cockpit Country.
"Land of Look Behind."
Trelawny.

89

■ Harvesting sugar cane.
Priory, St. Ann.

90

■ Sugar mill at Gray's Inn Estate.
Annotto Bay, St. Mary.

92

● Folly Ruins.
Portland.

93

■ Old stone wall with
rolling hills.
Lumsden - St. Ann.

● Blue Hole and white villas at
San San Bay.
Portland.

95

■ Old sign post on
Bog Walk Road.
St. Catherine.

● Admiral George Rodney
Memorial, erected in the late
eighteenth century.
Spanish Town, St. Catherine.

97

■ Old plantation houses at
Hector River Farm.
Portland.

● New Kingston.

99

Jamaican residences.

Acadia Gardens, St. Andrew.
Liguanea, St. Andrew.
Mandeville, Manchester.

Beverly Hills, St. Andrew.
Liguanea, St. Andrew.
Irish Town, St. Andrew.

100

● Cherry Garden.
  St. Andrew.

101

Rose Hall House.
"Home of Annie Palmer."
St. James.

■ Court Houses.

Mandeville Square.
Manchester.

104

● And at Morant Bay with
statue of National Hero Paul
Bogle.
St.Thomas.

105

■ Clock at Old Harbour Square.
St. Catherine.

106

● Water fountain at Sam Sharpe
Square, Montego Bay.
St. James.

107

Transportation.
"Any Style."

Bog Walk Gorge
Spanish Town Road   Wakefield   Red Hills Road

Spanish Town Road.

■ Looking east towards Mocho
Mountains near Mandeville.
Manchester.

● Crossing the Flat Bridge over
the Rio Cobre River.
Bog Walk, St. Catherine.

111

Ships and boats.

Ocho Rios
Morant Bay

Negril
Kingston

Ocho Rios
Hellshire Beach

● Looking west toward
Hopewell from Montego Bay.
St. James.

113

■ Sunset at Negril.
Westmoreland.

THE PEOPLE

The original inhabitants of the island were the Arawaks, a tribe of Indians who sailed from the Guyanas and Venezuela to settle in Jamaica around 1,000 A.D. Small, well-shaped with straight black hair, these simple, primitive people fared poorly under Spanish rule. By 1655, the entire race had been wiped out. This created a gap in the slave labour force which was fundamental to the immense sugar industry. In the years spanning 1673 and 1739, Jamaica had burst on the scene as the world's largest sugar producer, increasing her sugar estates more than six-fold. In the process, however, an interdependent need was created between the slave and sugar trades: neither could flourish without the other. Thus the stage was set for the importation of African slaves to Jamaica. After slavery was abolished, immigrant workers were introduced from the Orient and East India, and, from Europe,

North America and the Middle East came merchants and people of other professions. Although their language, culture and customs differed, they were able to blend easily into the Jamaican lifestyle.

A smattering of early church missionaries were the only ones to show sympathy for the slave's lot and these often fought to better their plight. Out of those early missionaries' efforts sprang a deep and abiding love for religion and to this day, it is the yarn that weaves the fabric of Jamaican life.

This was also a time when "obeah" flourished - that most harmful of religions transported from Africa with the slave trade. The obeahmen were all-powerful and even today their influence has not been totally stamped out. In some parts of Jamaica, there are still practicers and believers of obeah.

Rastafarians, named after Ras Tafari, Prince of the House of Tafari in Ethiopia, have their own religion. Believing Haile Selassie to be the Messiah of the Black People, their credo rests on the concept that salvation for the black man can only come through repatriation to Africa. Despite their unusual looks, the Rastafarians wish only to lead a life based on peace and love.

Some of Jamaica's most interesting architectural relics are churches - many of these dating back to the seventeenth century. There are also some ultra-modern ones, built with open-air concept so that voices raised in song and prayer can be heard clear and sweet throughout the countryside.

Sports also have a special place in the hearts of Jamaicans. Cricket heads up their list of favourites, with horse racing being a close second. Almost every young Jamaican boy dreams of growing up and representing his country on the West Indian Cricket Team. Few are chosen - but many dare to hope. When visiting teams come to play in Jamaica, thousands jam Sabina Park - and as many thousands in the streets have transistor radios pressed to their ears.

In the mornings, groups of city children wait noisily for their buses to take them to school, wearing uniforms which tell you more about the schools they attend than the actual names. In the country, there is no rush to get to school and many stop to "stone a mango tree", books balanced precariously on small heads.

Like in every other country, Jamaicans have traditional dishes prepared in a manner unique to the island: ackee and saltfish, curry goat, curry chicken, jerk pork, pepper shrimps, escovitch fish, roasted breadfruit, johnny cake, rice and peas made with coconut milk, and mackerel run-down.

The patois is another unusual aspect of the islanders. It is a mixture of Elizabethan English, African, Spanish, Dutch and Portuguese - diverse heritages coming together in a common dialect.

There is a strong cultural movement in Jamaica, supported by talented painters, sculptors, poets and songwriters who overcame many barriers to create things uniquely Jamaican. Self-expression comes in other forms: theatre, pantomime, pocomania, Jonkanoo - from the John Canoe dance which started back in the slave days -

modern dance as taught in the respected School of Modern Dance and, of course, reggae. The tragic death of Bob Marley, the prime mover and promoter of reggae, was a loss felt by everyone who had ever been exposed to the fiery passion of the man and his music.

No editorial on Jamaica would be complete without a last mention of the inter-relation between the land and the people. Jamaicans are nourished by the warm ground beneath their feet, the caressing rays on their bodies and the breathtaking settings. These have a way of soothing them spiritually, fostering a contentment with the world around them. In many ways, this explains their inherent friendliness and artless approach to problems: "Soon come" or ... Don't rush, things will fall into place in their own time. Accept this philosophy and you, too, have entered the mainstream of Jamaican life.

Mother and daughter.
Kingston.

125

126

Young faces in Jamaica.

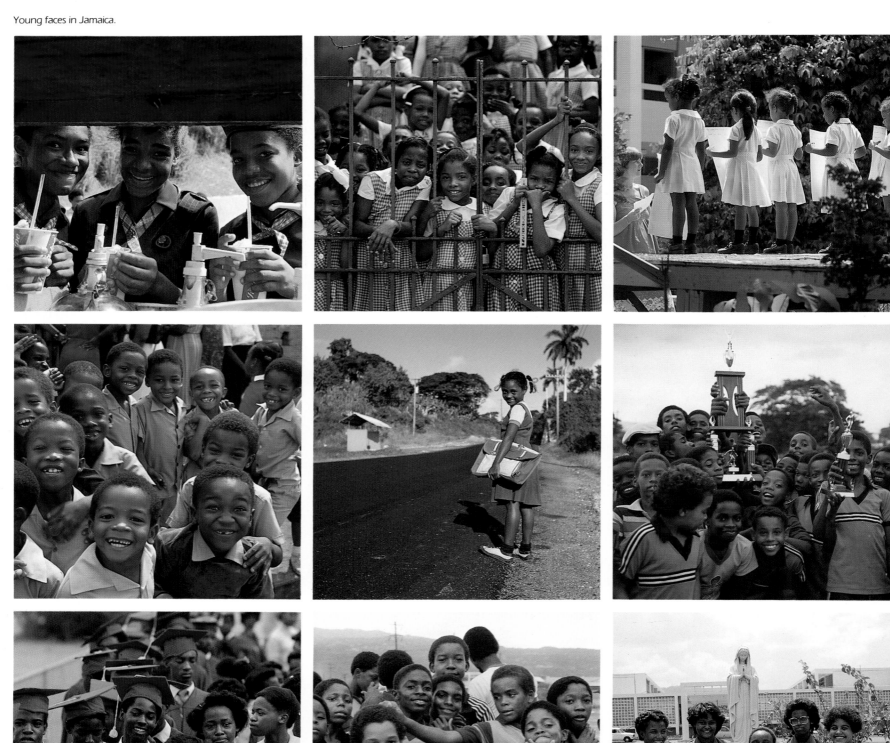

Celebrating at the
National Stadium.
Kingston.

129

Class portrait at
Nightingale Grove.
St. Elizabeth.

130

"Friends."
Spanish Town.
St. Catherine.

131

Three generations.
Woodland, St. Elizabeth.

132

"Family."
Kingston.

Sunday morning dip.
Ocho Rios, St. Ann.

134

"Gone Fishing."
Ocho Rios, St. Ann.

135

"Big Splash"
Swimming in the
Diver's River.
Portland.

Taking a dip on washday in
the Rio Cobre River.
Crescent District, St. Catherine.

Sunday morning service at
Walderston.
Manchester.

Altar boys of
Holy Cross Church.
Half-Way Tree, St. Andrew.

Baptismal ceremony at
St. Peter and Paul Church.
Rev. Kenneth Mock Yen with
proud parents of twins.
Liguanea, St. Andrew.

141

Church bonnets.

142

Churches.

St. Peter's Church.
Alley, Clarendon.
Holy Cross Church.
Half-Way Tree.
Holy Trinity Cathedral.
Kingston.

St. George's Church.
Annotto Bay.
Kingston Parish Church.
Kingston.
Christ Church. Port Antonio.

Manchioneal Anglican
Church. Manchioneal.
Methodist Church. Porus.
United Congregation of
Israelites. Kingston.

144

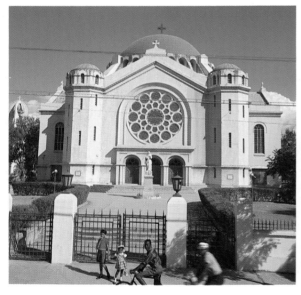

145

Worshippers under tent.
Kingston.

St. Mary Anglican Church.
Long Bay, Portland.

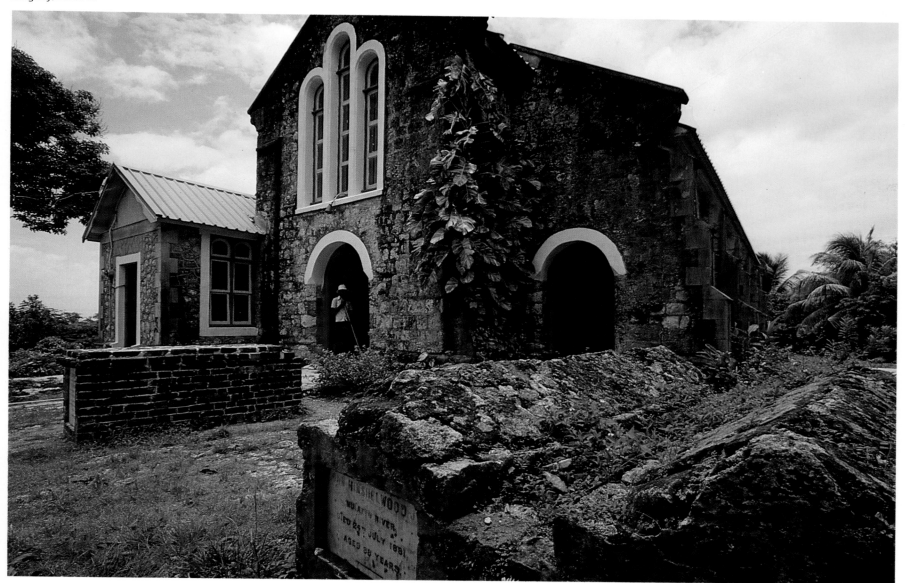

147

Interiors -

Trinity A.M.E. Zion church.
Port Antonio.

Holy Cross Church.
Half-Way Tree.

Zion Episcopal Baptist Church.
Kingston.

United Penticostal Church.
Ocho Rios, St. Ann.

149

"Hallelujah."
"Praise The Lord."
Zion Episcopal Baptist.
Bamboo.
St. Ann.

150

Kingstonians' favourite beach
and meeting place.
Hellshire Beach, St. Catherine.

"Festival and Fry fish,
Bammy, Lobster, and a
Red Stripe."
Hellshire Beach. St. Catherine.

153

Bathing beauties.

"Young Travellers."
Falmouth, Trelawny.

Jamaica Defence Force
helicopter pilots.
Kingston.

157

"Sisters."
Old Harbour, St. Catherine.

158

Wedding.
Ocho Rios, St. Ann.

159

Faces of Jamaican women.

Jamaican youth.

161

"A Day at the Races."
Caymanas, St. Catherine.

162

Country road
Orange Park, St. Thomas.

Polo match.
Drax Hall, St. Ann.

Cricket Time.
Kingston.

"Cricket - Lovely Cricket."
Sabina Park, Kingston.

167

Colourful shades.
Lacovia - Tombstone.
St. Elizabeth.

168

"Barefoot Runners."
Crescent District, St. Catherine.

169

Boys at work and play.

Kingston
Caymanas - St. Catherine

Berrydale - Portland
Kingston

Kingston

170

Enjoying a good guinep.
Kingston.

Syrup for sale.
Montego Bay, St. James.

172

Peanut Vendor.
Linstead, St. Catherine.

173

Market place.
Brown's Town, St. Ann.

174

Market places.
Port Maria, St. Mary.

Colorful Catadupa cottons.
Catadupa, St. James.

178

Harvesting Okra.
Clarendon.

180

Selecting the best yam for
market.
Lorrimers, Trelawny.

Rafting on the
Rio Grande River.
Portland.

182

Wash day.
Rio Grande River, Portland.

183

Rastafarians and their art.

Ocho Rios, St. Ann
Montego Bay, St. James

184

"A Happy Face."
Rio Bueno, Trelawny.

185

"Side-walk vendor"
Kingston.

186

"Friends of Andy Capp."
St. Ann's Bay. St. Ann.

"Appleton Rum."
Kingston.

188

"Water Lane."
Kingston.

189

Domino break.
Kingston.

190

Enjoying jerk pork and
chicken.

Reach Falls.
Portland.

193

"Cool Water."
Kingston.

194

195

Red Ponciana.
Montego Bay, St. James.

196

"Going-out."
White Horses, St. Thomas.

198

Old Harbour Bay fishermen.
St. Catherine.

200

"Coming-In."
Bluefields, Westmoreland.

"Fish vendors."
Hope Wharf, Westmoreland.

Squid for supper.
Port Antonio, Portland.

203

Fishing scene.

Morant Bay
St. Thomas.

White Horses
St. Thomas.
Lucea, Hanover.

204

Morant Bay
St. Thomas.

Fishing.

Lucea, Hanover.

Faces.

And more faces.

"John Canoe."
Kingston.

"A Celebration."
National Stadium, Kingston.

209

Jamaica Defence Force in
ceremonial dress.

210

Jamaica Military Band.

Jamaica Police Academy.

Recording sounds at Aquarius
Studios.
Kingston.

214

Limbo Dancer
Ocho Rios.
St. Ann.

216

Artists and Sculptor.

Albert Huie
George Rodney

Kay Sullivan
Barrington Watson

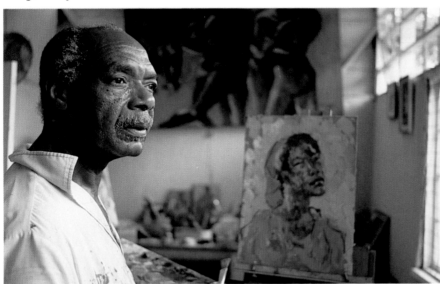

"Kapo."
Bishop Mallica Reynolds
Artist - Sculptor
Religious leader and family
man.

219

Laura Facey - Cooper
An artist and her work.

"The Story Teller." Miss Lou.
The Hon. Louise Bennett-
Coverly.

221

"Pantomime"
On stage at Ward Theatre.
Kingston.

Fashion show.
Montego Bay.
St. James.

223

"REGGAE SUNSPLASH"
The morning after an
"all night" music festival.

224

225

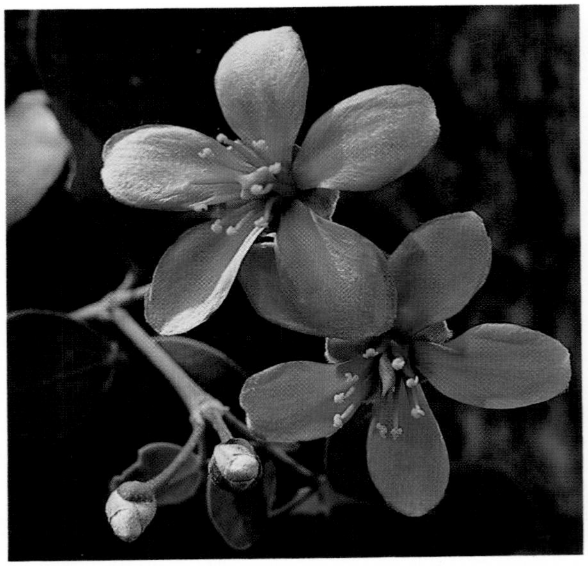

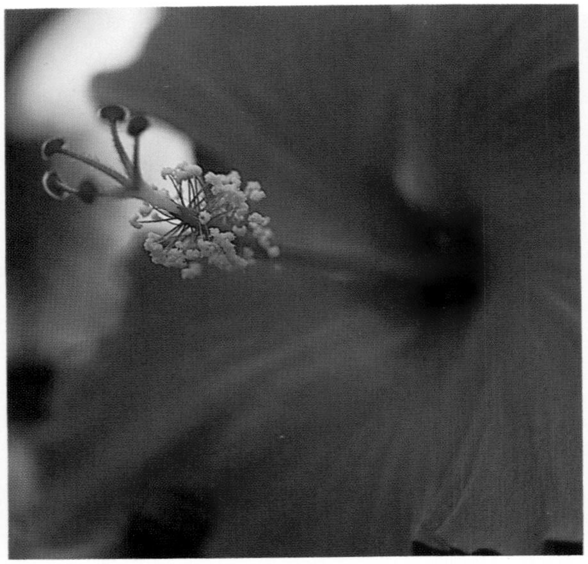

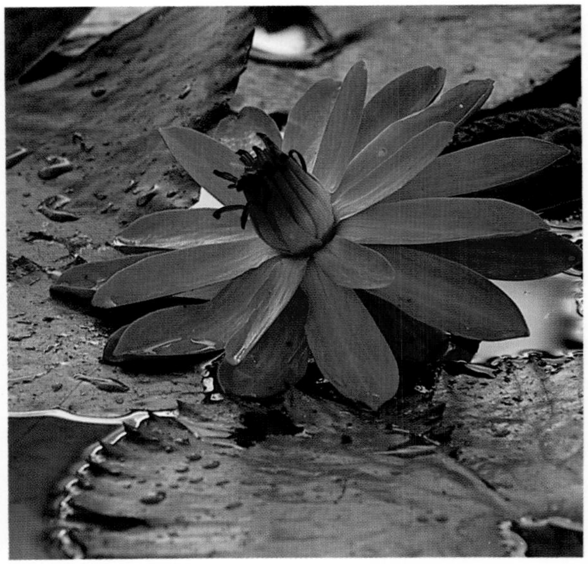

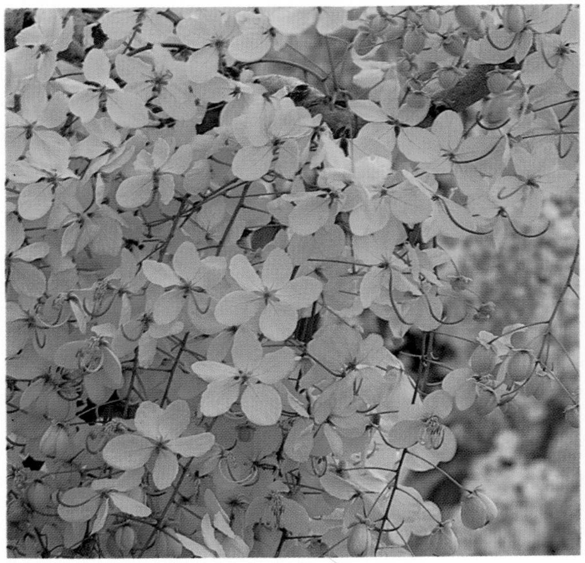

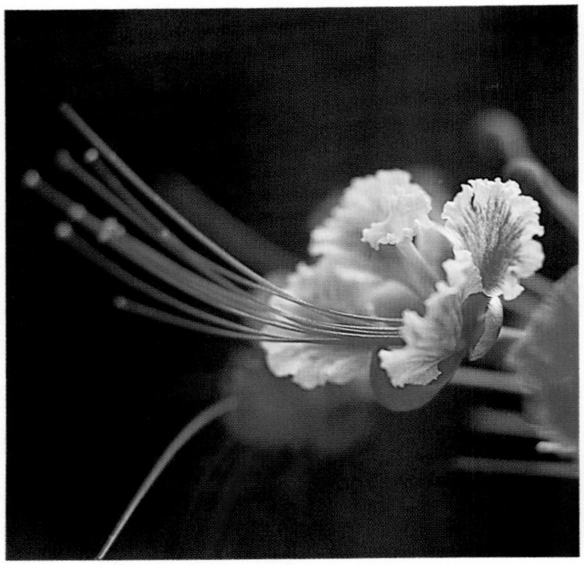

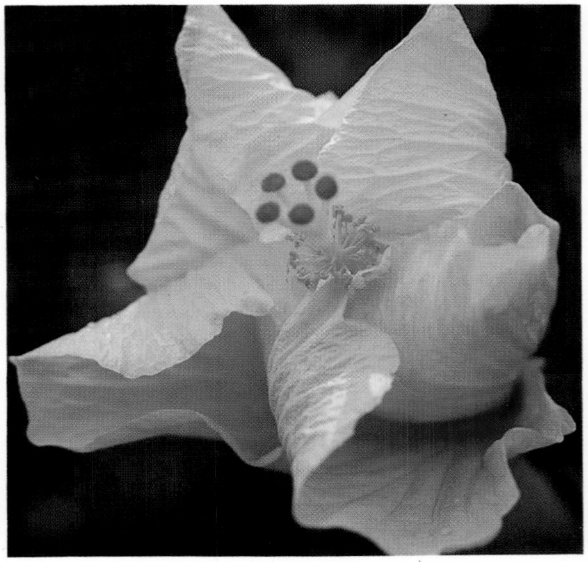

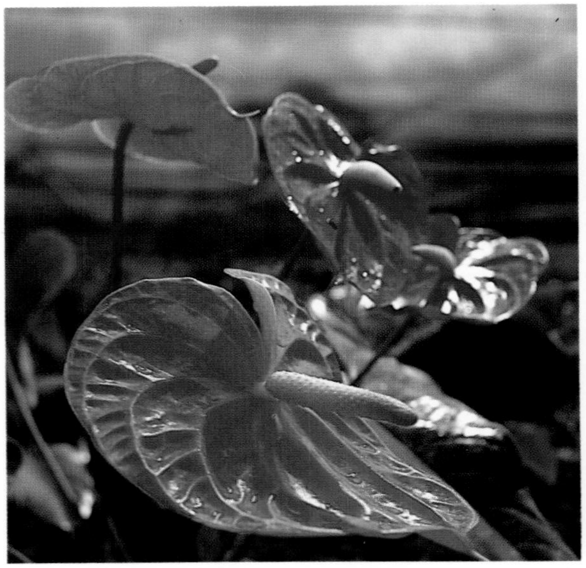

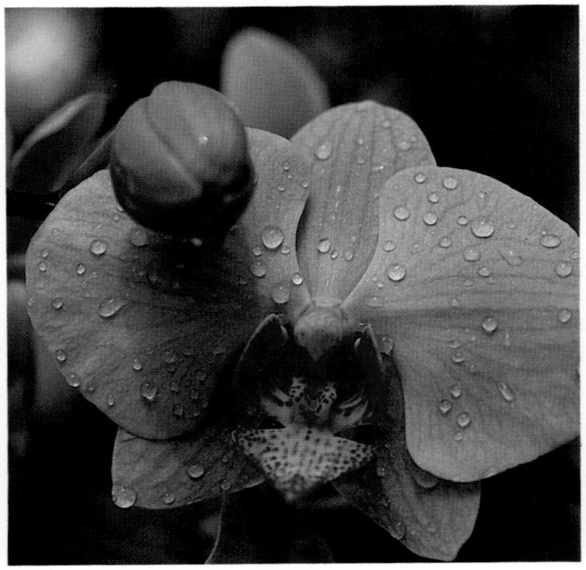

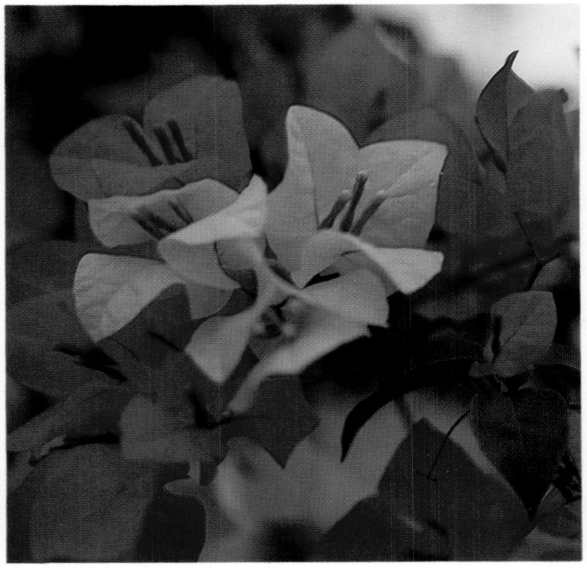

and food of Jamaica.

Signs of the times.

228